# RESTORED FAITH

DIANE HASTINGS

WESTBOW
PRESS®
A DIVISION OF THOMAS NELSON
& ZONDERVAN

WestBow Press books may be ordered through booksellers or by contacting:

WestBow Press
A Division of Thomas Nelson & Zondervan
1663 Liberty Drive
Bloomington, IN 47403
www.westbowpress.com
844-714-3454

ISBN: 978-1-6642-1789-8 (sc)
ISBN: 978-1-6642-1788-1 (e)

Library of Congress Control Number: 2020926012

Print information available on the last page.

WestBow Press rev. date: 01/19/2021

# CONTENTS

# ACKNOWLEDGEMENTS

Thank God the Father for the glorious and wonderful things that he has done for me. I thank him for his resurrection power and his love for me. I thank him for my mother and for my late husband who supported me in whatever I was doing. I thank God for my children, grandchildren, and great grand-children. I thank him for my sister, Paulette Davis who encouraged me to write, and sent me books and literature on writing and self-publishing. I thank God for Lydia Gonzales and other church and family members who encouraged and supported me through the process of writing and living for God. I give God all the Glory for my life.

# INTRODUCTION

This book is written for those like me, who have been in a spiritual battle of tests and trials that seemed to be long and drawn out. You thought you were coming out when all of a sudden you sunk deeper into the test. Your faith was shaken and you felt like things were never going to get better. You begin to live with just getting by day by day, and expecting that God was soon to come and you didn't have long here on earth. You were settling with what you were dealing with.

Beloved God has great things in store for you. You don't have to be complacent or taken down by anyone. You are the light of the world. You are the child of a king. 1 Corinthians 2:9 KJV says "But as it is written, EYE HATH NOT SEEN, NOR EAR HEARD, NEITHER HAVE ENTERED INTO THE HEART OF MAN, THE THINGS WHICH GOD HATH PREPARED FOR THEM THAT LOVE HIM." So, stand up, speak the word of God, study the word of God and trust the word of God. He is a faithful and loving God. He is ready to restore your faith and trust in Him.

# BEGINNING OF FAITH RESTORED

The title of this book is "Restored Faith". I named it that because, sometimes during our Christian walk our faith gets weak or we lose faith because of our life circumstances. Even, when we are doing everything we know to do, we still, sometimes, get weary. Which is why the bible tells us in Galatians 6:9 KJV "And Let us not be weary in well doing: for in due season we shall reap, if we faint not." If you get faint hearted along the way, don't give up. Remember what God's word says, because in due time we will reap the harvest, if we faint not." Quitting is not an option. Winners never quit, and quitters never win. You are a winner.

I looked at the definition of restored, it's meaning showed me, "giving back or returning; recovering from ruin or decay; repairing: renewing; replacing; reinstating; healing; reviving and curing. To be restored or renewed means you once was whole, complete, sound, healthy, etc. When you restore a piece of furniture, sometimes you have to strip, sand, buff, paint or varnish it to bring it back to its original beauty. As a child of God, you also have to go through molding and shaping to be what God wants you to be. It doesn't always feel good to go through the different stages of being renewed or made over. But, the longer you stay on the potter's wheel or in the fire praying and trusting God, the better you will be.

Let us look a little closer at being stripped from everything that is not like God. First God strips us of unrighteousness, then the sanding and the rubbing to get the rough areas that are still left in our lives. After we go through all of this then comes the buffing, smoothing, polishing and varnishing to give us the gloss and protection, which is the Holy Ghost.

This is all part of the process of being restored back to God and faith, when you have lost your way. Sometimes, you can lose hope and your faith, when you get weak and take your eyes off of God. I lost my faith because I felt like I had been lied to, betrayed and deceived. Even though God was showing me dreams and revealing things to me, I was being lied to about the situation. I was angry and bitter. I just wanted to quit and give up. I didn't understand why these things were happening to me. I would say to God, 'all I want is to be saved.' I don't want to hurt anyone and I don't want anything from anybody. I would go to church and go home.

If someone needed help and I could help them, I would and then return home. At times, I was miserable. I felt like I couldn't breathe. The depression, oppression and suppression were so strong, but real. I would pray to the Lord to let me lay down and not wake up. That's just how bad my situation had gotten. I was so tired I began to tell God how tired I had become. I would ask him what was my purpose?

He was listening, but he never gave me an answer or a word at that time. He never told me why I was going through this particular thing or why it was being allowed to happen to me, especially by someone I trusted in. He kept telling me to teach, and I would say yes. But all of the time my mind was focused on my circumstances. I had all the right tools to push through.

But I just wanted to give up. I didn't want to fight anymore. So, I planned my exit, when all the time God would be saying no to me. Deep down inside the Lord was still tugging on me, even when I wanted to let go. He would have me encouraging someone else with a scripture, a hug, a prayer or putting money in someone's hand, when I didn't even have a job.

I would think I'm messed up and in serious need of help myself. I thought how could you help someone when you are the one that needed help yourself. But GOD, was keeping and sustaining me. I wanted to just fade out of the picture, altogether. But something on the inside was still there pulling on me and I would hear different songs flowing through my mind, ministering to me. I would go to bed and wake up hearing the same song still in my memory just as fresh as it was when I was sleeping.

I knew that God loved me. I was just tired, frustrated and very disappointed. I felt as though I didn't have anything or anyone. My children are grown living their own lives. And Covid-19 took my husband and other people only called me when they needed something. They were pulling on me and draining me for what they needed.

I felt out of touch with life. So, I tried volunteering and serving with the Red Cross and the Salvation Army. That worked for a little while. I was trying to make my life exciting and fulfilling, trying to fill the void and stay occupied. But the depression was still there.

I knew I had to get back in right standing and communion with God. The real connection wasn't there. I was just going through the motions. And yes, I prayed and read my bible, but something was off and I knew it.

I knew being in right standing with God was where my help was coming from. I had been so spiritually beaten up and hurt by some family members and church folks that I backed away from a lot of them. I didn't trust anyone. I was leery of everything. I didn't realize that when I backed off of things, I was the one losing out because I also got distance from God.

I had lost fellowship with him and that caused my weakness and downfall. No matter what you go through, always stay in right standing with God and never give up hope. God is always there. He will never give up on you. John 10:28 KJV tells us "And I give unto them eternal life; and they shall never perish, neither shall any man pluck them out of my hand". Isaiah 54:17KJV "No weapon that is formed against thee shall prosper; and every tongue that shall rise against thee in judgment thou shalt condemn. This is the heritage of the servants of the LORD, and their righteousness is of me, saith the LORD". You have the victory through Christ Jesus.

No one or thing can separate you from God, only you can separate yourself from God and His love. Trials and tribulations are going to come and go, Jesus has overcome them and the world. If you trust the Lord and have faith and hang in there, no matter what, the Lord will see you through. He will restore you. Our God is a faithful God. He will complete what he has started in you. Because God is faithful to His promises. Numbers 23:19 KJV says, "God is not a man, that he should lie;neither the son of man, that he should repent: hath he said, and shall he not do it?or hath he spoken, and shall he not make it good?" God can not lie. If he said that he will do it, then stand on his word, because it's coming to pass. He will restore your faith, your hope, your joy, your peace, your strength and give you the reassurance that you need.

The Bible tells us that we will suffer persecutions and have tribulations, but we have an advocate and an intercessor that stands in the gap on our behalf. Trust in the Lord and don't give up.

Life happens, it is how we deal with it and what we do that will determine our outcome. Will you go through complaining or will you go through victorious? We already have the victory through Christ Jesus. 1 John 4:4 KJV says, "Ye are of God, little children, and have overcome them: because greater is he that is in you, than he that is in the world."

If you have lost your faith or your hope, then I ask you to reconnect to the true vine, which is Jesus Christ the hope of glory. Revelations 3:20 KJV says, "Behold I stand at the door, and knock: if any man hear my voice, and open the door, I will come in to him, and will sup with him, and he with me." God is waiting on you and me.

He sent Jesus his son to prepare a place in heaven for all those who will accept and receive his gift of salvation. We will all have to come before his throne. God is knocking, will you answer his call?

Time is winding up. It's time to seek God while he may be found and call Him while he is around. There may be a time when he won't be reachable. Call and seek him now. Don't wait because it might be too late.

He's coming like a thief in the night. Give God a chance to restore your faith. His word promises to restore what was lost. He has compassion for you. He will pick up the pieces from the places that have been scattered. It doesn't matter how far you've fallen or how wide spread you are.

God is able to come get you from wherever you are. He promises to bring you out of the land that your ancestors possessed. Hosea 6:1 KJV says, "Come, and let us return unto the Lord: for he hath torn, and he will heal us; he hath smitten, and he will bind us up." God wants to heal the broken hearted and mend us. We have to ask him to and then let him, because he won't go beyond our will. He gave us free will.

Now, since God gave us a free will, we must take back what the enemy has stolen from us, whether it be your joy, peace, happiness, finances, relationships, your marriage or your strength. You must fast and pray and take it all back.

If you make one step God will make two. He just wants you to be willing to take that step. Even, if it is your health, take it back. Remember what the word says in Isaiah 53:5 KJV "But he was wounded for our transgressions, he was bruised for our iniquities: the chastisement of our peace was upon him; and with his stripes we are healed". We are delivered and set free. In Jeremiah 29:11 KJV it says" For I know the thoughts that I think toward you, saith the Lord, thoughts of peace, and not of evil, to give you an expected end". God wants the best for His people. He doesn't want anyone to be lost or perish. So, repent and turn away from anything that is hindering you and that is sinful. Trust His word, seek God's face, pray for restoration: Pray that God will renew, revive, heal, restore, refresh and bring you back to Him.

# RESTORATION/RESTORED

Restoration comes from acknowledgement that you are in need of a savior, repentance, praying, and seeking God's face. To be restored you have to have already been saved and back slid or are on your way back into the world.

This means somewhere down the road of your spiritual journey you got weak, gave up, or something tragic or horrific happened in your life to cause you to give up hope. This is where three of the gospels in the new testament comes into play, when it uses a metaphor about the conditions of the heart. It is the scripture about the sower sowing seed and some of them fell by the wayside, some fell upon stony places, and some fell on the thorns; but others fell on the good ground.

When the word of God is not rooted in your heart it is easy to slip away from God's hand, because you don't have what it takes to stand. It's the word that will keep you. It's the word that you can use to call to God's remembrance. It's the word that you can look to for guidance and instructions. The bible is your road map to life. When you have the word of God rooted in your heart nothing can shake you. Psalm 119:11KJV says, "Thy word have I hid in mine heart, that I might not sin against you." Mathew 24:35 KJV says, "Heaven and earth shall pass away, but my words shall not pass away."

God's word stands forever and that is what you need to stand on when life circumstances happen. God has given so many signs in the Bible by using prophets and other saints to tell us to pray, turn back to him, to repent, to get rid of idols, to seek his face and more. The reason he is giving us the word and these instructions is because he loves us and he is soon to return.

He knows that we are in need of a savior and restoration. That is why he sent his son Jesus Christ to redeem us. But, we as a people are sometimes stubborn, hard headed, disobedient, carnal minded, wavering, and we straddle the fence and have gotten lukewarm.

We need to turn back to God, our first love. We need to be restored, our priorities, motives, hearts, and minds have to be turned back to God. Somewhere down the line we have gotten off track. This is why I will explain some of the things that can take your focus off of God, his promises and doing the will of God.

We all know that we are going to have tests and trials. And, we are aware and look for those things to happen. But it is the subtle, underlying, small foxes that we don't notice that creep in and rock you to the core. This is when restoration is much needed. All you have to do is repent and go to God.

He is waiting for you. In 2 Peter 3:9 KJV His word tells us that "The Lord is not slack concerning his promise, as some men count slackness; but is longsuffering to usward, not willing that any should perish, but that all should come to repentance". His word tells us in Ezekiel 18:4 KJV "Behold, all souls are mine;

as the soul of the father, so also the soul of the son is mine: the soul that sinneth, it shall die." In St. John 3:16 KJV His word tells us that "For God so loved the world, that he gave his only begotten Son, that whosoever believeth in him should not perish, but have everlasting life." That shows us that God loves us and we can be restored.

God has made the way available to us. He can pick you up from wherever you are and refresh your soul. All you have to do is ask him, believe that he is able to do it. Stand on his word and pray through the process. Don't faint, don't give up. Stand on the word of God and what it has to say about your future and the promises of God that is on the way. God is on your side and you can't lose with him.

Romans 8:31 KJV says "What shall we then say to these things? If God be for us, who can be against us?" In Romans 8:38 &39 KJV Paul tells us, 38"For I am persuaded, that neither death, nor life, nor angels, nor principalities, nor powers, nor things present, nor things to come," 39"Nor height, nor depth, nor any other creature, shall be able to separate us from the love of God, which is in Christ Jesus our Lord." Let him revive you and bring you back into the ark of safety with him. We already know that in him is the safest place to be. So, turn around, recommit and walk into your destiny. God is waiting!

# BROKEN

Being broken is one of the signs that you need to be restored. When you are broken, sometimes you feel like the wind has been knocked out of you. Everything you attempt to do always winds up in failure. You have been hit so many times that you feel that there is no more wind in you or no regrouping from where you have fallen.

Every time you make one step forward, you fall back two or three steps. Your world is filled with darkness and gloom. You smile or laugh, but deep inside you are suffocating, wondering can they not see the position I am in, and the pain that I feel? Do they not know that I need help? Sometimes you walk around in zombie land, just existing. It's like you are on a treadmill, walking slowly not getting anywhere and everyone else is moving forward, but not you.

You're standing and watching others advance or move on in life. You questioned, why am I in this state when all I want to do is live holy in the Lord and serve Him? What is going on with me? Some people walked by shaking their heads or having disappointment on their faces. But none have prayed and asked God why does this person look like they are in a daze or what happened to them?

There's a difference in being broken for God and being broken by the enemy. God convicts and woos you back to him. The enemy condemns you and points the finger at you. When you are broken by God, he is making you and preparing you for ministry. When the enemy breaks you down, he leaves you for dead, in hopes that there won't be any chance for recovery.

God's word said I won't put more on you than you can bare. His word said I will not leave you or forsake you. When you feel like all is lost and you can't make it or feel like you can't breathe, look up and see Jesus.

David said in Psalms 121:1 KJV that "I will lift up mine eyes unto the hills, from whence cometh my help". We know from experience and from scripture that the Lord is our help. You are never alone and you will make it, if you hang in there and not faint. Our adversary wants you to faint. But, don't faint. In Galatians 6:9 KJV it tells us "And let us not be weary in well doing: for in due season we shall reap, if we faint not". You might be broken for now. This too shall pass. God is restoring the broken in heart. My words to you are to trust God, don't faint, and don't give up. Change is coming!

# SHATTERED

Sometimes things come into your life that can shatter you. When something is shattered it is crushed or broken into so many pieces that it's hard to find all of the pieces or hard to put back together. Sometimes the pieces are all over the place, which is how it feels to be shattered. You have been crushed so many times by different ones. Every time you turn around it's a hit here and a hit there. You begin to wonder if you have done something wrong. Each time an attack comes if you are not praying sincerely or already prayed up. They chip at you more and more and cause you to get weaker. If you begin to call on the name of the Lord and reposition yourself spiritually, you will be able to pick yourself up out of that shattered place. It does not matter how scattered you are. God can put every little piece back g together.

Just like the very hairs of our head are numbered. God knows where every piece goes. When you get shattered, you feel damaged. Remember what Paul said in 2 Corinthians 4:8 & 9 KJV it says "8 We are troubled on every side, yet not distressed; we are perplexed, but not in despair; 9 Persecuted, but not forsaken; cast down, but not destroyed;"

We might be shattered into many pieces and don't know how we're going to get back together. But we have an advocate, Jesus, who is standing in the gap and praying and interceding for us every day. He is just waiting for us to decide whom we will serve. So, it's time to put the pieces back together again. You can do it by calling on the name of the Lord for help.

When Peter was walking on the water he started to sink, and when he realized that he was going under he began to call on the Lord, asking him to save him. That is when Jesus reached out his hand and lifted him up. The Lord is waiting for us to call out to him. His word says in Jeremiah 33:3 KJV" Call unto me, and I will answer thee, and shew thee great and mighty things, which thou knowest not, and also in Isaiah 65:24KJV "And it shall come to pass, that before they call, I will answer; and while they are yet speaking I will hear." God is waiting.

The Lord is the lifter of our heads. Sometimes we look for other people to put the pieces back together for us. God is standing right there to help us. When you are weighed down with heavy burdens and problems you can go to him in prayer. He will give you what you need. He knows how to give us the rest and peace that will bring us out of our situations.

You don't have to be shattered any longer. God has greater things in store for you. He wants to give you peace, not evil. He wants to give you a good end. So, pick up every little piece of your life that is shattered and begin to let God mend every part and put it back in the right places.

# CONFUSED

When you are walking around living in confusion this is another sign that you need your faith and your mind restored in the Lord. Sometimes confusion can come from things like stress, being tired, or other things. MedlinePlus Encyclopedia states that, "confusion is the inability to think as clearly or quickly as you normally do. You may feel disoriented and have difficulty paying attention, remembering things and making decisions." The enemy will have you thinking that no one cares or that they don't see you. And all the time that, you are having these thoughts about others. They themselves are dealing with something that may be heavy. It might not be the same as you, but they are going through. They may come in with their head hung down or have a smile on their face, to keep from crying. They may need encouragement and prayer, also. The enemy will have you thinking that it is for another reason. That is just one example of the way he causes confusion. He will have your mind thinking the wrong things. If you would just reach out and talk to the person you will know that they need you, just as much as you need them. And that what you were thinking wasn't as it seemed to be. You might have even been confused about your relationship with the Lord, feeling as if He didn't do what he should have done. That he should have kept a loved one around or that you should not be going through the things that you are going through.

In Isaiah 55:8 KJV it tells us" For my thoughts are not your thoughts, neither are your ways my ways, saith the Lord." God knows what he is doing and He has our best interest at heart. He knows how to show forth his power. If we would take the time to study God's word and search the scriptures, we would know his character. We would know what the word says concerning us, what pertains to us and his promises, then we won't be confused. If you are having a problem with your brothers or sisters and it's causing confusion, you need to go to them and talk about it. Then you can clear up anything that you were confused about. After you get everything cleared up, pray and bind the enemy out of your relationship. Once that is taken care of you can focus on your road to recovery. When you can stop the enemy from keeping up confusion and discord in the body of Christ, or just in yourself. You will have accomplished something wonderful. When we change our thinking about negative situations or things we think are out of order, we can be on the road to seeing things positive.

If you focus on negative things long enough it will affect your actions and the way you live your life, your thoughts, your mind, your actions will also become infected with negative vibes. So, if we think about things that are positive, we won't be so confused and uptight about everything. We already know that God is not the author of confusion, but he is a God of peace and love. When you have any of these thoughts, that are negative and not like

God, rebuke them. God wants to restore you. He wants you to be healthy. He wants you to prosper in every area of your life. Let us let our minds be like the mind of Christ Jesus, and there will be no confusion. You can be free in the Lord.

# ABUSED

Abuse is a terrible thing. It will have your emotions and heart all mixed up. That is another reason you need restoration. You can be free in the Lord. If you feel abused by being misused, mistreated or even insulted., remember that God loves you and he will never abuse or mistreat you. Sometimes we feel abused, because people take us for granted or they take our kindness for weakness. Someone may have abused your love or friendship, because you treated them kindly. So, they go a little farther and assume that you were supposed to do the things that you do. When you are in God's care. You don't have to worry about being abused. He will watch over you and warn you. The Bible tells us that we are not ignorant of Satan's tricks. God will take care of you. Of course, you have to remove yourself from abusive relationships and situations. Sometimes we can put ourselves into things that can cause people to take advantage of us. Pray that God will give you the wisdom to know what's best for you. Abuse comes in many forms, sometimes it's physical, mentally, emotionally and even verbally.

God wants us to love one another and treat each other right, with love and respect. Some people want to keep their distance from you. When they do, you should still speak kindly to them, go your way and pray for them. You can't make people love you or want to be around you. When you have been abused or wounded, you have to forgive them, pray for them sincerely, the way the bible says to pray and move on. Don't let this be a shadow over your head, move on. The enemy tries to torment you or hold things over your head. Pray and ask God to help you to love with an unconditional love and give you wisdom. You won't be misused or abused anymore.

You have to pray because sometimes certain situations cause you to be drained or your emotions are all over the place. That is the trick of the enemy to keep you all bound and bottled up. Release it and let it go. Give it to God and be free from everything that makes you feel disrespected, ill-treated, violated, depressed or down in your spirit. John 8:36 KJV tells us, "If the son therefore shall make you free, ye shall be free indeed." When the Lord sets you free, you are free. The Lord can make you free from abusive situations.

Some relationships can be very toxic or abusive. You need to recognize these toxic relationships and move on. Toxic relationships can be dangerous and they can cause you to be frustrated and drained. Don't let toxic or abusive people keep you from experiencing all that God has for you. Refocus and redirect your attention on God. He will see you through. God has a better plan for your life. This is what restored faith is all about. When your faith is restored you can trust God again. You'll wait and let him send the right people into your life. That way you won't experience a lot of hardships, because you and your mate will be on one accord.

# FAITH

Faith is the thing, if you have it, that will help you to the next level in your life. You need it to receive restoration. "Faith is belief, trust or reliance especially to a higher power," according to The New Unger's Bible dictionary. "It deals with a relationship between God and man. In some respect, correlation, for man's faith which responds to and sustained in God's faithfulness." Faith is an action word that requires you to make a move or act on what you believe. Faith is unseen. You can't feel it or touch it, but you know it's there.

Paul tells us in the book of 2 Corinthians 5:7 KJV "(For we walk by faith, not by sight:)" In Hebrews 11:6 KJV, it tells us "But without faith it is impossible to please him: for he that cometh to God must believe that he is, and that he is a rewarder of them that diligently seek him." So, when you are believing or trusting God for another chance, stand on his word. If you are trusting him for healing or deliverance be assured that God is faithful to all of his promises. He can not lie and will not lie. He will perform those things that he said he will do. His word tells us in 1 John

9 KJv, "If we confess our sins, he is faithful and just to forgive us our sins, and to cleanse us from all unrighteousness." Have faith In God and know that he is standing and fighting on your behalf. God is the best lawyer and judge to have on your side. He has not lost a case yet. He's working on your case and mines.

With God in our corner we will win, because the victory has already been won. Once you give your life to God, you automatically become a winner. And if you are a winner you just have to walk into your destiny and call that was planned for you by God and keep standing in God.

Yes, you are going to go through some trials and tribulations. That is a promise to all of us. We know if we live a Godly life, we will go through persecutions. If we suffer with him, we can also reign with him in the end. Even runners and winners have to condition their bodies to prepare for the race. So, run your race and cross the finish line to get the gold medal. I trust that you will stay in the race and finish. There is much more for you on the other side. Isaiah 40:31 KJV says "But they that wait upon the Lord shall renew their strength; they shall mount up with wings as eagles; they shall run, and not be weary; and they shall walk, and not faint." Do you believe that God is able to fix your situation? If so, invite him in and watch him do it for you.

# DISTRACTIONS

Distractions are other ways that prove that you need to be restored and your mind renewed. The enemy uses distractions to take our attention off of our assignments, off our mission and off of God and the plans he has for us. Distractions come in many forms. Sometimes you can recognize them and sometimes you cannot. When you are easily distracted, it just means that it is time to renew your mind. Philippians 2:5 KJV says, "Let this mind be in you, which was also in Christ Jesus:" This means we have to think like Jesus. When Satan tried to tempt him, he never got distracted. Jesus spoke the word and stayed his course.

Distraction causes you to run into unnecessary problems and you can even get into dangerous situations, because you are not paying attention to your surroundings or circumstances. Distraction means that your full attention is not on a person or thing and that something or someone is preventing you from focusing. "The synonyms of distraction are diversion, interruption, disturbance, intrusion, interference. obstruction and hindrances". From (Google searched) If you see any of these synonyms in your life pertaining to distraction, you need restoration of your mind.

God is able to restore you and move every hindrance and distraction. Distractions come all of a sudden, unexpectedly and without any warning. When it does just refocus on what is important and what is right. If you still don't know, God is able to move every hindrance or distraction. His word tells us to set our affections on the things that are high above and not on the things on this earth, not on the hindrances or distractions, not on one's self or abilities. But on the God who is able to give us whatever we need. When you find yourself distracted, just remember what the word says about thinking on the things that are true, honest, just, pure, lovely, and of a good report. In other words, the beautiful and peaceful things in life. Don't let distractions get in the way of you receiving restoration.

# RESTORED FAITH

**N**ow that you have been through all of the struggle of being broken, shattered, confused, distracted, misunderstood, etc. You can see clearly that God was with you all along. He was bringing you back to him through every trial. He was in the midst of it all. You couldn't see him or what he was doing, because your judgments and your views were clouded with life.

Sometimes things can come back to back that knock you off your feet. You don't know which way you're going. And when God gets a hold of you things suddenly begin to change. Those feelings of anger and hurt begin to change. A burden lifts off of you. You begin to relax and release every problem to God. You realize that God really does have you.

We forget God when the problems and situations arise. Because we are in some tests for long periods of time. Then we tend to try to work through it ourselves, without God. Which causes us to mess it up even more or cause us to be in the situation even longer. We forget the scripture in Philippians 4:13 that says,

"I can do all things through Christ which strengtheneth me." or the song, "Without God I can do nothing."

God is trying to renew and restore our faith in him. God is causing your joy to be restored, your peace to be restored and your faith to be restored, and built upon. He is stirring up things in you that were once buried. Renewing your heart and renewing your mind, putting laughter back in your spirit again, where there was dread now you have reassurance and anticipation.

Where your dreams had died, he is awakening them again. Arise men and women of God. Go back, pick up your sword and shield. Put on the whole armor of God. The battle is not over, it's just beginning. God is refreshing you again. He is putting new light and a new fire in you.

Rejoice for God has restored your faith in him and he has strengthened you for the next test or journey that is before you. I know it might not feel like it, but we don't operate by feelings. We operate by faith, and the word of God. Feelings say I can't make it. God's word says, "I can do all things through Christ which strengtheneth me. Philippians 4:13 KJV" Feelings say I'm going to die. God's word says, "I shall not die, but live, and declare the works of the Lord. Psalm 118:17KJV" Feelings says I'm sick, God's word says, "But he was wounded for our transgressions, he was bruised for our iniquities : the chastisement of our peace was upon him; and with his stripes we are healed. Isaiah 53:5 KJV"

Trust God and his word. His word says, Isaiah 43:18 &19 "18KJV Remember ye not the former things, neither consider the things of old. 19 Behold, I will do a new thing; now it shall spring forth; shall ye not know it? I will even make a way in the wilderness, and rivers in the desert".

You see God is doing this thing not us. He is bringing you through your wilderness and desert to get you back on tract and back with him. Psalm 23:3 KJV tells us that, "He restoreth my soul: he leadeth me in the paths of righteousness for his name's sake."

Jeremiah 30:17 KJV For I will restore health unto thee, and I will heal thee of thy wounds, saith the Lord; because they called thee an Outcast, saying, This is Zion, whom no man seeketh after."

If you look back over your life, you will see that you have come a long way. You are not where you want to be, but you are not where you used to be. Keep pressing toward God and don't give up. God can deliver you from whatever is stopping you from drawing closer to him. He can restore you again, if you will let him.

# CONCLUSION

The conclusion is this, God is a restorer to all that will receive him. So receive him that you may be the one that he calls his sons and daughters. There is no place that he can't reach you. There is no problem or situation that you may have that God can't bring you out of. He is all seeing, all knowing and forever present. He is ready and willing to come to your rescue. All you have to do is ask him.

Many times, the people of God were in trouble and when they called on the name of God, he heard their cry and brought them through their situation. God is merciful, loving, long suffering, patient, and faithful. Psalm 46:1 KJV says, "God is our refuge and strength, a very present help in trouble." You can call him when you need him, and call on him when you don't. He's always there. Keep the faith, and have faith in God.

# ABOUT THE AUTHOR

Diane M. Hastings is a native of St. Louis, Missouri, raised in East St. Louis, Illinois. Diane is an author. Her first book was, "There is Help in the Midst of Your Trials." She loves reading, singing, using her tablet and working with her hands. She currently resides in Colorado, Springs, Colorado. She has seven living children and many grand-children and great grand-children. Diane loves the Lord, and knows that the Lord loves her. She knows that no matter what happens in her life, that there is nothing too hard for him to do. She knows that her God is a faithful God to every promise that he has said. Diane, also knows that God will finish the work that he has begun in her.

# REFERENCES

The New Unger Bible Dictionary, Revised and Updated Edition 1988, Additional and New Material Copy

New Webster's Dictionary and Roget's Thesaurus, Copyright 1991, 1992, Ottenheimer Publisher, Inc. 1997, Landoll, Inc.

Vine's Expository Dictionary of Old & New Testament Words Published in 1997 by Thomas Nelson, Inc., Nashville, Tennessee

Vine's Expository Dictionary of Old & New Testament Words Published in 1996, which copyright is now restored by the Gatt Treaty to W.E. Vince copyright, Ltd., Bath, England

The International Standard Bible Encyclopedia, copyright 1988, Wm. B. Eerdmans Publishing Co., 255 Jefferson Ave. S.E Grand Rapids, Michigan 49503

The Zondervan Pictorial Encyclopedia of the Bible, copyright 1975, 1976 by Zondervan.

King James Version, Copyright 1990 by Thomas Nelson, Inc.

Google Search

MedlinePlus Encyclopedia – Article on Google February 27, 2018